Beyond Our Kennel

I was born in Newington Green, Islington, and moved to Luton while still incontinent. There I spent my childhood, accompanying my family on my father's retirement to Bristol where I did Biology, Economics and English 'A' Levels in flared trousers. After a year's break, during which I realised my childhood ambition of being a bus conductor, I attended Bradford University and got a degree in European Literature and the History of Ideas and Sociology, and a degree of aptitude in making curries. I then returned to London and began working in children's theatre. Some friends advised that my sense of the whimsical might be appreciated at a late-night comedy venue. They were wrong.

D0417280

For my old dad

Also by John Hegley

JOHN HEGLEY

Beyond Our Kennel

Methuen

Published by Methuen in 1999

1 3 5 7 9 10 8 6 4 2

First published in hardback in the United Kingdom
in 1998 by Methuen Publishing Limited

This paperback edition was first published in 1999
by Methuen Publishing Limited
215 Vauxhall Bridge Road, London SW1V 1EJ

Peribo Pty Ltd, 58 Beaumont Road, Mount Kuring-Gai
NSW 2080, Australia, ACN 002 273 761
(for Australia and New Zealand)

Copyright © 1998 John Hegley

John Hegley has asserted his right under the Copyright, Designs
and Patents Act, 1988, to be identified as the author of this work

Methuen Publishing Limited Reg. No. 3543167

A CIP catalogue record for this book is available from the British Library

ISBN 0 413 73210 X

Typeset by SX Composing DTP, Rayleigh, Essex

Printed and bound in Great Britain by
Cox & Wyman Ltd, Reading, Berkshire

Caution
All rights whatsoever in these poems are strictly reserved and application
for performance etc should be made to: Peters, Fraser and Dunlop,
503–4 The Chambers, Chelsea Harbour, Lots Road, London SW10 OXF.
No performance may be given unless a licence has been obtained.

This book is sold subject to the condition that it shall not, by way of trade or
otherwise, be lent, resold, hired out, or otherwise circulated in any form of
binding or cover other than that in which it is published and without a similar
condition, including this condition, being imposed on the subsequent purchaser.

Contents

Three

One

A Boy's Best Gift

One day when I was seven or so
I told my dad of my desperate desire for a Christmas dog.
And he said 'No no no no no no no no no NO. NO!'
It didn't look too good.
'Why do you want a dog anyway?'
'Because I have no friends.'
'But you've got Tony. Tony's your friend.'
'Tony was my friend and then he got a dog,
    now his dog's his friend.'
'I'm sorry John, no dog and that's the end of it.'
That Christmas my dad got me a kennel.

After the initial bewilderment
I crawled inside and became the very dog I had requested.
I became my own best friend.

The Luton Bungalow

Not counting the goldfish which we didn't really know
there were five of us in our family in the Luton Bungalow.

My brother loved the aeroplanes
that lived up in the sky,
any love that you could get
you didn't let go by
and he hung around the airport
where they had a good supply
of aeroplanes.

My sister was no plane spotter
she much used to prefer
the wings of the theatre
I made specially for her.
The characters were cardboard
and the action rather slow
but she cried as Mister Punch was hung
in our Luton bungalow.

My mother was of Kentish stock
from Ramsgate by the sea
and she cleaned the place around the clock
and around the settee.
She cleaned the household surfaces
like she had to get below
the surface of existence
in the Luton bungalow

My father's mother she was French
and he was from Paree
and I like to think of my father as
the Luton Fleur de Lea
Simon de Montfort may have lived in Luton long ago
and he may have stood on a higher rung
but he had no bungalow.

When my father became angry
there was lather there was foam
at the corners of my father's mouth
but still it felt like home.
I would hit my sister
then someone else hit me
then all of us went down the church
to say that we were sorry.
The Lord gave us forgiveness
then all of us would go
back for further beatings
in the Luton bungalow.

Poem About My Sister

My dad told my sister not to play with her food.
It was reasonable advice,
carrots do not make very good friends.

Poem de terre

I'm not a normal person
whatever that may be
there is something very very vegetable
about me,
this human skin I'm skulking in
it's only there for show,
I'm a potato.
When I told my father
it was something of a blow,
he was hurt
and he called me a dirty so-and-so.
He kicked up a racket
and he grabbed me by the jacket;
I said, 'Daddy will you pack it in
I need you for my father not my foe
Daddy, will you try and help me grow,
won't you love me for my blemishes
and look me in the eye
before one of us is underground
and the other says goodbye?'
And he said, 'No'.

When I was a schoolboy
I never knew why
I was so crap at cross-country running
but now I know
why I was so slow.
I'm a potato.

The Deliberable Mistake

Once again my sister had been insufficiently competitive
in our living room board-gaming session
and after a brief chase into the kitchen
I had gone to kick her,
but being no good at football
misjudged the move
and connected with my mother's leg instead.
Hearing the commotion, my dad hurried in from the
    shed.
'He's deliberabley kicked me in the varicose vein,' she
    said
and my father's eyes spoke
of the calibre of beating which was to follow.
My explanation that I was aiming for my sister
was not seen as a mitigating circumstance.

Tucked up in Bedfordshire

The first bit of pornography I saw
was in Luton's main Co-operative store
when I was maybe seven.
it was on a surprisingly low shelf
and when I got home, I got closer to heaven
by holding on to the image
as well as onto myself.
Later in the week
I went in daily to scan
the pictures, avoiding skilfully
the peek
of the assistant,
although as a man
I have become more resistant
to such titillation
as I find it tends to make you
imagine people
continually bending over
all ready for action
which is a bit of a distraction
when you are trying to see them purely
as footballers.

The Beatles in Our Luton Bungalow

With the Beatles about
you had to admit
that it got better.
They put a hum
into the humdrum
and the drab.
Those four made us glad to be alive.
They made the five of us feel fab.
They were one of the three things
our family could appreciate together.
The other two were sleep
and oxygen.

A Londoner's Lament

I was formed in Luton
but in London I was born
and now I live in London
that's where I woke up this morning
and I went down to the bus stop
to catch a seventy-three
and to a bloke stood at the bus stop
I said, 'Have you been waiting long?'
And e-ven-tu-a-lee
he said, 'That's my business mate'.
London's got an attitude problem
and a problem with the air
it's turned into a motorkazi
can you help us Tony Blair?
There's things that's wrong with London
they ain't what they used to be
there's things that's wrong with London
and there's things that's wrong with me,
but here we're concerned with things that's wrong with
     London,
the sick city that only BUPA can recuperate?
High-rise prices, low-rise cardboard,
cheapo cider, port and starboard.
But out of work and murky as it is
the big river remains a quivering life-giver,
the city retains something for the enthusiastic siever:
the culture, the multiculture,
the architecture, the parkitecture,

the spark of fellow feeling, it's still there,
there's plenty left to wave at
as well as that which ought to drown
maybe it's because I'm a Londoner
that I love Luton Town.

Love in Luton

I was three or four when I lost my heart
to a boy on the telly with a vital part
in a cowboy show called Laramie
I'd go to bed and imagine he was there with me.
I'd give a big kiss to the one I'd seen
in the scheduled slot
on the little screen.
When my primary schooling had begun
I fell in love with a nun,
I was yet to reach the common fear
of saying what I meant
and I bent her ear,
'I want to kiss you sister,' I told her straight,
'Thank you, John,' she said, 'that's great.'
Then she added that she was spoken for
by the word of God
and I spoke no more.

More Love in Luton

At ten I loved Jane but was frightened to say
and I suffered frustration throughout the school day
I kicked at her ankles, it rankled and bought
attention but not the affection I sought,
the strength of my feelings I couldn't admit
and out of my weakness I acted the git
and my acting was good.
Then Wojtek appeared in a neighbouring seat
he said that her writing was lovely and neat
he said that her being was really complete
and this she preferred to the ends of my feet.
Wojtek and she became chummy and close,
it churned up my tummy, it made me morose.

Back at the bungalow lacking delight
I blurted the hurting at dinner one night,
I said how I loved her and it wasn't right,
explaining how Wojtek was deeply preferred.
As soon as I'd spoken my ear got a pull
from my dad who said, 'Wait 'til your plate isn't full
before you start speaking,' I answered, 'It's not
plate, Dad, it's mouth,' and he said, 'Oh yes, sorry John,
    I forgot.'
So letting my family in on my grief
didn't provide a great deal of relief.

Now looking back on the burden and pain
of unspoken feeling congealing for Jane

I feel that some justice was done for the way
I treated my sister
to loads of dismay.
I was very unchristian
but still went to church,
a fan of the man
who was pinned to the perch,
I served on the altar
spoke Latin aloud
and so did my brother,
my mother was proud
of us knelt in our white and our black,
I held the incense
my brother, the slack
of the thing with the holes that created the stench
and back home my father tried teaching him French,
my father's first language, my father's first son
and one extra lesson when praying was done.
But one day the Sunday tradition was broke
why, I'm not sure, but my dad never spoke
in the language thereafter, except for the day
when his mother came over and then went away,
we had no exposure to uncles and aunts
my dad's only friends were his God and his plants.

Away from Home

In Bristol at first I missed Luton a lot
Rovers and City for me they were not
a viable substitute, I was bereft
of the little in Luton I'd recently left.
But, doing my A levels I would become
the class entertainer and I found a chum
with a sense of the comic the same as my own
I was Lutonless, yes, but no longer alone.
My A levels over, I put on a tie,
I worked in an office, a government guy
and then on the buses accepting the fares
relaxing in trousers so glad to be flares.
I did meditation, I looked to the East
my father got worried and spoke to the priest.
We argued so often because I was not
what he would call normal, his favourite slot;
once I came home after ringing my bell
and my father said; 'How many times must I tell
you, John, please hang your coat up, it's not a hotel,
and I turned and I thumped him and over he fell.
I helped him get up into one of the chairs
and I begged him to say he had fell down the stairs
And he answered 'All right', with a bump on his brow
'But it's lucky we're not in the bungalow, now, John.'

College Days

I study philosophy, mixing with fellows
who mix their own muesli
and listen to cellos.

After Schooling

With college days behind me I am signed up by a team
for taking care of kids who do not care for normal
  schooling,
the arrangement is informal and the purpose of the
  scheme
is to try to keep them occupied and keep them out of
  fooling
round the avenues of Bradford, once, we did a horror
  play
with me the crazy scientist and they the living dead,
after laughter at my madnesses a zombie lad would say
that I was useless as a teacher and should try the stage
  instead
And I would think you're right, but I've not had the
  education
I haven't been to drama school, so I have missed the boat
but I'd learned that you can learn outside the usual
  location
from the kids, which gave me comfort as I went to get my
  coat
out of the dustbin.

Into Entertainment

With hope of an opening
some kind of stage door
I go with guitar down to London once more
and someone will say there's a vacant position
for an actor/musician in children's theatre.
I do an audition and I get a letter
which opens the way and my eyes become wetter,
a kingdom a stage and a bright yellow sweater
and someone will say that my whimsical verses
have wider potential and should be allowed
a hearing in front of the comedy crowd.

The comedy crowd's had a belly of beer,
it seems pretty base but I get the idea
gold from the dross, it is possible here,
the job is to hold in the palm of my hand
the future
the mob
and the microphone stand.
I climb on the stage with my nerves all on end
it isn't a problem if I can pretend.
I get on the altar,
I open my heart,
I falter at first,
then they pull me apart.

Mything My Father

When my dad went
when all his time here was spent
I was out of the country and not to be found,
not around for his requiem.
He would have been so annoyed,
even the one mass he would have got me to
I managed to avoid.

Long since my father's departure,
a distant diocese
an unexpected holiness,
a holiday in Greece.
A high place on an island,
rugged and remote
with something for the traveller with something to
    devote.
The closing of the afternoon, a little church of white
inside there are candles, although none is set alight.
There's sand inside a metal stand, where candles have
    been lit
but they must have fallen over after burning for a bit.
I pay a hundred drachmas
put my flame upon the wick
and remember how my father used to make me rather
    sick
with his far too frequent asking if I'd had the time to light
a candle in the time since I had been out of his sight.

The candle I set light to now
I set alight for him,
beeswax I imagine
and exceptionally slim.
I'm about to leave the chapel
when I think I'd best be sure
that the candle hasn't fallen
like the others had before.
That's when the myth of Orpheus arises in my mind,
the one about the geezer who went underground to find
Eurydice, the deal is she can follow him from Hell
or Hades as they called it, he can have her mortal shell
and her soul as well
as long as he does not look back, it's going very well
he's almost overground
and then what does he do? That's right he looks around.
Perhaps a sudden doubt,
whatever it was, I never bothered turning
to discover if the candle for my daddy had gone out
and once out in the open I accepted he had gone,
the myth had been my guide
and I knew his light would burn beyond
the one I'd left inside.

Two

The Happy Mistake

One night I heard another poet say
'omelette'
when he had meant to say
'Hamlet'.
I wish him well with his gift.

Mental Health Poem

When he went out of his mind
we helped him find
the key to get back in.
It was behind
the dustbin.
The one that had it in for him.

Changing Channels

Television doesn't turn me on
there was a time when it did
when it was flickering constantly
but now that time has gone
and the telly's gone out of the window;
you're just there to be controlled
it wants more attention than a two-year-old,
you're food for the telly
when you're glued to the telly
I've cast my telly
and I've cast my vote,
it's so remote.
I've sat there talking to the telly all day
but they never seem to listen to a word I say.
I look at my hands and think whose are they?
If you don't like it, what do you do?
Send an opinion to *Points Of View*?
I've got rid of that box of tricks,
and Jim'll never fix it, now.
I took hold of the telly
and I took aim
I took care not to damage
the window frame,
that hasn't done anything, has it?
Well, it has, actually,
but that's another story.

Some People

Some people write their names in books
even when they're thirty-three and they only
live with one other person.
Some people shake sugar sachets for longer than need be.
Some people sniff a pint of milk
even when they only bought it today.
Some people say, 'God is that that the time,' when they
    don't believe in Miracles.
Some people give you a retractable biro
retracted, and some with the nib nosing out.
Some people check their appearances in car mirrors.
Some people think they are more important than they
    are.
Some people look around in their bag
without knowing what they're looking for.
Most people pull down towels in public toilets surplus to
    their needs,
a few push muck up into the unrevealed towelling.
Some people do not understand how seeds become plants
    or trees.
Some people dig deep into supermarket mushroom heaps
so as not to get any touched by other people.
Some people heap their salad bowls to stupidity
when it's a serve-yourself establishment
but rarely do these people go back to their place
and make their heap carefully into a map of the former
    Yugoslavia.

Alien in Rouen

I've escaped to a school in Normandy
to lustre up my lingo.
The other students are mainly from Japan,
small, quiet and companionable.
One morning a new pupil appears
he is a rugged giant of a man.
In the break for our coffee,
broken words through missing teeth
tell me that he is a Bosnian refugee,
he is unemployed and has joined the class
to turn his situation about.
He could knock you into the semaine prochaine
if he gave you a clout,
but he reads and writes French like an infant.
At the blackboard the professor
teaches him how to spell the French word for without.

French Potato Poem

Voyez, voyez, la pomme de terre
c'est le légume que je préfère,
ce n'est pas une carotte ou un haricot vert.
Non!
Ce n'est pas le légume ordinaire,
c'est le premier
et la première.
L'existence sans la pomme de terre
c'est comme le poisson sans la mer
ou comme le train sans chemin de fer
c'est la joie pour moi la pomme de terre
pour lui aussi,
l'homme derrière.

The Fan

The man came up to me after the show
because he wanted me to know
that the poem about my dog being dead
had moved him.
'My dog died yesterday
and what you wrote helped me out,' he said.
'I'm not a poetry man
but that was OK.'
He told me how the expression of grief
for my own dog's curtains
had given him a certain relief.
There were feelings which never quite came to the surface
after he'd dug his dog under the surface.
'It's just a shame,' he added,
'that the one in your story never had the same name as
    mine.
Perhaps you could change it for me,' he said,
'otherwise things might get a bit nasty'.

An Aeroplane Journey

He threw it at her in school assembly. He had assembled it during the sports notices. A page from the hymn book. It was her look he was after. Her look.

In his lap he flipped the tightly printed page into the tightly folded plane. She was in his head ninety-five per cent of his waking day and sixty-five per cent of his dreaming night. Sometimes he'd wanted to scream his fat infatuation when she was near and sometimes he'd wanted to whisper it in her ear so gentle. Instead he'd put his energies into keeping a stifled mask of no interest whatsoever. Fear of rejection? Of just fear? Whatever it was, it was fearful. Now he was going to throw down the mask. He was going to let the throwing of the plane do the asking. 'How about a date? You're great!' he'd written in the top margin and signed it.

Heads down for silent prayer; he knew that would be his moment. He took careful aim.

Fly! fly little arrow to my heart's desire. To the source of this fire, fly, fly little arrow down a narrow corridor straight to your target. And the air was ridden and the message ended up where bidden. Silent, swift, unnoticed by the sundry and the all, falling, nestling in her spectacles. She took hold of the piece of paper and immediately caught sight of the handwriting so boldly put upon the wing. The name was a shock for sure. His dissembling had covered up his wonderment so well. She hadn't been able to tell a single bubble of the cauldron burning up inside him. But she knew now. She knew just how the chemistry master felt about her. And she was a very happy head teacher indeed.

Cabin Crew

Yesterday
I spoke to a bloke
who was a purser with BA.
He was gay.
Probably still is
I'd say.

Into Rail

The first train I rode in I rode in when I was eight
it was a beautiful beast, a great
one-nostrilled, black dragon
cheerfully dragging its human wagon loads.
Now the nostrils have gone
but the benevolence goes on.
The loco lives
the loco gives.
Even the trains
I do not catch
transport me.

Lost Going to Shropshire

Just out of Euston
on a trip to Shrewsbury
changing at Crewe
the announcement, 'If anybody has lost anything
please contact the guard at the back of the train.'
I like the ambiguity,
just as I like the ambiguity in art, dance and poetry.
Passengers invade the vestibules
to check their luggage.
I imagine a queue forming at the train's back,
with various lostnesses:
I've lost a glove.
I've lost a gland.
I've lost fourteen nil at blow football in my time.
I've lost the ability to live purely in the moment.

Unseeing Sense

Changing train and track
on the way to Blackpool at Preston
I mount the awaiting connection
and get settled in an empty block of four
adjacent to a man similarly situated,
but in a dodgier mac
who looks at me for longer than is generally deemed
     acceptable.
Behind me, a labrador-led passenger
is assisted on to the service
by an official who lodges him
opposite the staring stranger.
The dog is eyed and then the owner.
'So how did you lose your sight then?'
he casually opens the chat,
dangerously to my mind.
'Oh, I've been blind since birth.'
'So you won't actually miss seeing then?'
'That's right,' answers the other
incredibly politely adjudge
in the face of this grudgingly graceless inquisition.
The dogless one looks out of the window
and absent-mindedly continues,
'They've done a good job with this station,
looks very individual, don't you think?'
'Er . . . yes . . . it's got a good feel to it,'
says the other, keeping cool and convivial
whilst giving his dog an unseen tug
which translates as
please urinate on my interrogator.

Pickering to Grosmont

From Pickering to Grosmont
you can go by steam
and that's what me and Nigel did
and it was extremely eye-opening.
Putting my head from a window
gave me a surprise
even with your glasses on
the soot gets in your eyes.
Further up another bloke
was leaning through a door
looking at the moor,
he wasn't bothered by the smoke
because of what he wore,
he wore underwater glasses
he'd done this before
and I said can I have a go
and he said are you poor?
I said not particularly
and he explained that he wasn't a charity
    organisation either.

A Doncaster Romance

Johnny was a journalist
who went right off his rocker
when he went across the Pennines
to report on women's soccer.
He went crazy the day that he fell
for a goal-scoring Doncaster Belle.
Her beautifully skilled ball control
took possession of his Accrington soul
and when he came to speak
to her after the training session
his interviewing technique
became no interviewing technique to speak of at all
and as he spilled the beans of his admiration
the Donnie lass
found Johnny bright and bonnie enough
and asked him if he fancied a stroll
around the stalls of the fascinating local market.
Johnny looked thrilled.
'On your own, like,' she joked with him.

Joking Apart

I haven't seen you smile in a while
but I'll try and do the trick;
we bring each other down in the mouth
but I am optimistic;
we're not getting on, but I know what's to be done
I'm going down to the joke shop
we're gonna have some fun.
I'm going down to the joke shop
our lives are going to waste
love was just a novelty
but it can be replaced.
I'm going to swap my money
for some imitation poo
and I'll just be joking
the next time I do the dirty
on you
and the X-ray specs
are going to show us what we failed to see,
I'm going down to the joke shop,
whoopee!

The Loss of the Doss Bags

We were so angry
when we got back from the pub.
Someone had obviously got into the tent,
seen our doss bags
and thought, Right I'll have those.
Maybe not those words exactly
and maybe there was more than one of them
but certainly not more than two hundred
I'd have thought.
Anyway we were miles from anywhere,
obviously more miles from some places than others
and there was obviously no chance of getting any more
   doss bags at that time of night
and we never had any spare blankets or anything
and we weren't getting on that well either
and it's not like a war that can bring people together
because it's only your doss bags after all.
So we thought, blow this for a game of soldiers
and we went back to a phone box
that Tony had remembered passing
on the way back from the pub
and we rang the police.
Yes both of us.
We were so annoyed that both of us wanted to join in
and it was absolutely ages before anyone answered
and when they did they didn't seem overly concerned
   about the theft
and they didn't want a description of the doss bags or

anything.
I reckon it was because the police stole them in the first
place
if you ask me!

Spud Games

If you're desperate for a dice
in a game of snakes and ladders
you could dot a diced potato
with a felt-tip pen
but you wouldn't get that nice
rattling sound you get when
you shake a proper dice around in a cup,
also if you're tyring to climb up
the ladder to escape the snakes of infatuation
a diced potato
is no substitute for a sense of self-worth.

Food Poem

Although I rarely eat meat
and would not want to promote the substance
I still like to go into the butcher's
to buy my cheese
even though I know
that cheese money and meat money
are not separated in the till.

Blessèd be dogs.
Blessèd be dominoes.
Blessèd be black-eyed beans.
Blessèd be greens.
Blessèd be grit.
Blessèd be trampled confetti.
Blessèd be spoons.
Blessèd be spaghetti.
Blessèd be garden trowels.
Blessèd be hot towels in curry houses
that are really hot flannels.
Blessèd be kennels.
Blessèd be lead pencils with or without rubbers.
Blessèd be scrubbers
which are sponge and scrubber combined.
Blessèd be letter boxes
litter bins
can-openers
tin-openers
and the openness between us.
(All one blessing.)
Blessèd be sneezing.
Blessèd be snowmen.
Blessèd be concern for other people's snowmen.
Blessèd be our limitations.
Blessèd be carrots.

God Helps Those Who Help Each Other

I was just out of the house
when I noticed on my shirt
what looked like dirt.
Actually it was some rubber glue
misplaced during some greeting-card joinery.
Not of a mind to retrace
to my place of residence to change my gear
I attack the cack with my thumbnail
but to no avail.
After purchasing my ticket
at the station
beyond the barrier I encounter
a plastic pail-carrying bucketeer
paging 'Help the Aged'.
I treat the aged to a one pound coin
and am cheerfully offered a round
yellow sticker as reward.
Of a sudden I have inspiration.
I take it
and stick it
over my slight but visible muckiness.
It would seem that I am cleansed.
Thank the Lord.

A Higher Hundredsman

Going home
from the hippodrome
the chief centurion bumps
into a diplomatic chum
just come back to Rome
after a stretch away.
'So how were they?' enquires the soldier.
'Nutters,' answer his friend, 'no joke
we had one bloke
whose philosophy was to do unto others
as you'd be done unto. Can you
believe it?'
'No?!?' splutters the military man,
'Follow that to its end
and there'd be no more cheering
charioteering deaths like I've just witnessed in the 'drome.
Let's hope it doesn't catch on
or the Roman way'll be gone.
By the way did you get that soap I sent you, Pontius?'

Getting Away for Easter

Did he prefer his humour blue?
How old was he before he knew
the earthly job he had to do?
How many sugars in his brew?
He never got to make a pew
nor had a sniff at sniffing glue
but possibly he liked a brew
and on occasions even threw
up over Judas and the crew,
he surely must have done a few
of common things that people do,
and had he known the people who
would claim his name would he have grew
increasingly less likely to
get really stuck-up good and true.

If Jesus was of human kind
with higher nature which defined
the end his father had in mind
I ask if he'd have hung about
to let the blood come flooding out
or would his task be to be gone
and leave the cross with nothing on,
would he have run from being racked
and done the disappearing act
before his hands and feet were tacked?

The word made flesh would he decide
'To let myself be crucified
foreknowing, would be suicide
and Lord knows that's a sin,
I'm not sure I can save the world
but God, I'll save my skin.'

Faith and the Football League

Upon the water he begins to walk
and he bobs about like a lump of cork
and with the ocean barely above his feet
the Messiah beckons and then in comes Pete,
but within a few seconds the worry gets voiced
and the bleating Pete gets completely moist
and the Lord pulls him out
like he's a drowning pup
and says, 'Walking on the water's like life
in the relegation zone,
you've got to have faith if you're gonna stay up.'

Tuna Day (for the USA)

I say tewna, you say toona
I say happy new *year*,
you say happy *new* year
I say Cuba is a democracy worthy of
   recognition and respect . . .

Auckland Hesisitation

Outside the high-street café
a man whose hair is grey.
A handsome man I can say.
Thirty-three maybe.
Forty-three perhaps. Like me.
I want to go out and warmly
and quietly tell him
to dye his hair.
Dye it dark.
Dye it black.
Of course I don't do it.
How many more of these
petty constraints can I live with?

King's Cross

It's been called a red-light district
the district round King's Cross
and the residents don't like it,
well some of them don't.
One bloke who resides under cardboard in a doorway
couldn't give a toss,
he's far too busy asking for a brew
or a few bob towards the fare back to Glasgow.
'Can you spare some social change?'

A Declaration of Need

I need you like a novel needs a plot.
I need you like the greedy need a lot.
I need you like a hovel needs a certain level of grottiness
to qualify.
I need you like acne cream needs spottiness.
Like a calendar needs a week.
Like a colander needs a leek.
Like people need to seek out what life on Mars is.
Like hospitals need vases.
I need you.
I need you like a zoo needs a giraffe.
I need you like a psycho needs a path.
I need you like King Arthur needed a table
that was more than just a table for one.
I need you like a kiwi needs a fruit.
I need you like a wee wee needs a route out of the body.
I need you like Noddy needed little ears,
just for the contrast.
I need you like bone needs marrow.
I need you like straight needs narrow.
I need you like the broadest bean needs something else on
    the plate
before it can participate
in what you might describe as a decent meal.
I need you like a cappuccino needs froth.
I need you like a candle needs a moth
if it's going to burn its wings off.

You Kneed Me in the Groin

You used to touch me here
in such a wonderful way
but not today.
In that other place
your lingering fingers
were deep sea divers
cautiously advancing
towards our breathtaking element.
Before this truthless trap,
before these silences without secrets
you used to trace out the map
of all the rest of me.
Perhaps we should have kept
on coming up for air
without the coming.
Before this numbing.
Of the plumbing.

Some Resolutions

Some resolve to give up on the smoking
some resolve to cut out all the meat
some resolve to get their trunks more regularly soaking
and some resolve to stop all the deceit.
Some resolve to solve financial problems
by taking up a life involving crime
and some resolve to give their ageing parents
more than just the fag end of their time.
Some resolve to have a hobby
some resolve to join a lobby
some resolve to clear up every jobbie
that their doggie does
and not go hosepipe crazy in the drought
and some of the aforesaid resolutions
dissolve before the Christmas tree's been put outside the
    door,
especially resolutions one and four.

The Hair of the Dog

Sometimes when I'm at home
I wrap some Sellotape around my hand
and I go around the carpet
picking up the hair of the dog.
I did it for the whole of last Christmas
or as near as damn it,
it was the happiest Christmas I've had in all my days.
They don't call me Sticky Back Jack for nothing,
they call me it for something.
Some folk like a joke others like to choke on a fag,
me I like to pick it up and stick it in a carrier bag,
I don't mean to brag
but I've got quite a collection.
Picking it up, sticky side down
jabbing and dabbing around.
Picking it up, sticky side down,
the black and the white and the brown.
Of course I get some little bits of extraneous stuff
like little bits of fluff and cheese and that,
but that don't worry me,
because when she's shedding her winter coat
in the early Spring
I like to get on down and do my hairy thing
and then I wrap it round my head
like I'm the King of the Carpet.
You've got to take your pleasure
and get your treasure
when and where you can.

I'm a hunter.
I'm a gathering man.

Three

Beyond Our Kennel

John looks at the shelter that's made for a pet
and tells his friend Tony, 'I think we could get
both of us in there I'm willing to bet,
but not very much I am wary of debt.'
Tony says, 'Why don't we give it a go
if we never try we're unlikely to know.'
So they enter the kennel, a convoy of two,
Tony observes, 'It's as big as an igloo.'
It's bigger than that as they're soon to find out,
it's bigger than Derby and bigger than doubt.
The kennel is ever so large
you can go for a trip in a barge.
The kennel continues beyond where it should
there's room to meander and room to be stood
and Tony says, 'Where did they get all the wood, John?'
There's room in the kennel for flying a kite
inside the kennel it's roomy all right
there's room for the kennels all over the world
there's room for a boomerang wilfully hurled by Hercules,
there's room for an ocean and room for a breeze
there's room for innumerable steeplejack trees
John says, 'It's roomy'
and Tony agrees.
Tony and John get up onto their shoes
and John says, 'This kennel could be Doctor Who's
dog's.'

Traversing the kennel they come to a train

steaming and teeming with people from Spain
some from Seville, but Madrid in the main.
The duo get on and they sit and relax
they both love a railway and up on the racks
there's loads of potaters in hessian sacks
they could be pesetas though, I could be wrong
but we know they're potaters before very long
because one falls on Tony from out of a hole
and Tone does a header and says, 'It's a goal.
I'm off to the buffet to purchase a tea
do you want something getting John?' 'Nothing for me,
unless you're not charging your usual fee?'
'This service is gratis, it's free of all charge.'
'I'll have a tea then and I'll have a large
scone with no butter and plenty of marge,
an egg and cress sandwich and if you can get
a paper I'll have one and one serviette,
some crackers and cheese and a chocolate cone
some Shrewsbury biscuits, a couple of doughnuts,
an apple, an orange, some grapes without seeds,
an old Roman flower pot, a street map of Leeds
and apart from a purpose I've no other needs.'
The fact that his friend has an unbuttoned fly
John brings to his notice and Tony says, 'Why?'
then goes to the buffet without a goodbye.
He does himself up as he walks up the aisle
making a few of the Spaniards smile
and because he has buttons it takes him a while.
The train is in motion and John is entranced
by a boil on a neighbour that needs to be lanced,
he tries not to stare, he tries only to glance
and while Tony is gone and he's stood in the queue

64

the ticket inspector comes ticketing through
and happily sings,
   'Happy journey to you
   happy journey to you
   happy journey dear customers
   from us in the crew . . .'
the first number finished, she sings them the next
the tone I've forgotten but here is the text
   'He lived in Aberdeen
   Mister McNaberdeen
   but he didn't feel very free
   'cos they didn't make him feel
   like a man in his bonnet
   like they did in bonnie Dundee.'
The inspector keeps singing her various bits
with all of her being but none of the hits
and the boil on the passenger suddenly splits.
As if it's a sign for the others to leave,
the Spanish all vanish and John wipes his sleeve,
and tells the inspector, 'You ought to have sung
something apart from that barrow of dung.'
The inspector is stung and she gets in a strop
'Just going round going clip clip clip
all day long without a stop
it's worse than being a workhorse
even that goes clip clip clop.'
The official's offended, she canters away
she's off to her stable and back to the hay,
John's disappointed, he'd hoped she would say,
'Your banter's fantastic let's go all the way.'
She takes it to heart and a part of her dies,
I can't tell what bit though, nor fathom its size.

Tony re-enters presenting to John
serviette, tea, paper, sarnie and scone,
'I ran out of cash, here, where's everyone gone?'
'You should have heard all the hullabaloo,'
John says, removing the lid from his brew,
'I wish that I had, but I had things to do,
along with the purchase I needed a poo.'
John says, 'It sounds like a bit of a lark.'
Tony says, 'That was a feeble remark.'
And all in a flash they are out of the dark
but they're still in the kennel, and they disembark
at a station that's furnished with only a hut
the kind you might find when you pitch and you putt
with a sign saying *Kiosk* and one that says *Shut*.
They're met by the mayor who gives them a bow
he says, 'Call me Gus, though I'm partly a cow
and partly Ken Barlow
but don't ask me how.'
Gus tells the spuds, 'You'll be made into chips.'
'We think it's time for the turn of the turnips,'
one of them answers, in spite of no lips.
The peelers arrive and they ask for the names
of the spuds and one answers, 'We've all got the same,
We're all called 'King Edward.'
'Look, stop playing games.'
'Alright then copper, address me as James
the eighth of Scotland.'
And then there's the sound of the clacking of shutters,
it comes from the kiosk which looks like a hut as
the man says 'I'm open', and Johns says 'Yippee,
Tony, I'll get you a takeaway tea.'

'And while you are up there d'you think you could see
if they've got any peanuts?' 'I will certainly not,
you're getting a cupper and that is your lot.'

The man at the till's the old testament God
he's wearing the beard but he's dressed as a mod
with a chip on his shoulder the size of a hod.
John wants to say, You're a miserable sod,
but instead he is civil and orders the tea,
'Two, milk, no sugar,' but God pours him three,
'You take what you're given and lump it,' says he,
lumping the sugar in copiouslee.

Joan of Arc enters.
She's sitting astride
a horse that is dog-like and blue as the tide,
John asks her, 'Were you aware that you died
for a God who has such a cantankerous side?'
Joan answers, 'Not til I'd already fried.'
Then turning to Tony she tells him 'Je t'aime'
whilst taking a moment to banish some flem.
'I want you to love me as well as you can,'
Tony concurs with her intimate plan
saying, 'Take off your armour and I am your man.'
Joan starts releasing the pieces of steel
as Tony tells Joan how she's making him feel.
'I am no longer on an even keel
and never again will I return to a world
that is so much more familiar but infinitely less real.'
It seems that the kennel's a place where you find
a world that improves on the one left behind
unless you're a spud then it isn't so kind.

Tony and Joan are all feverish now
Joan gets her kit off and Tony says, 'Wow!
What star sign are you,' and Joan says, 'The Plough.'
Divested of fashion they touch and explore
swelling their passion to fill every pore
and then they start thrash'n
around on the floor.
When things become quiet John brings them the tea
and says, 'It's as well I have purchased the three.'
Joan has a sip and then tips it away
and turning to God she says, 'What are you playing at
answer me pray?
It's as cold as a stone not as hot as the sand,'
God says, 'It's your fault, you left it to stand'
and Joan says, 'How come you can make a world in
    seven days
but can't make a cup of tea
that'll stay hot for fifteen minutes?'

John gives his glasses a bit of a clean
and finds there's some scone from an earlier scene.
The mayor says, 'John, is it skon, skoan or skoon?
And am I the Milky Bar Dog of Dunoon?'
John doesn't answer
and doesn't discuss
and in pulls a driverless double-deck bus.
John doesn't like it and kicks up a fuss,
'Firstly they took the conductors away
now it's the drivers, I'm drove to dismay'.
The mayor of the kennel says, 'Son, it's OK
dogs aren't like people they don't get annoyed
if they're arbitrarily made unemployed,

organised labour's a thing to avoid.
To dogs automation is totally fab,
the driverless carriage the driverless cab,
of course there's the husky but he is a scab.'
The horse that brought Joan then chips into the chat,
'If you want to travel and want to be sat,
come sit on my saddle I'll make you my load,
I'll happily take you to Kenilworth Road.'
(Luton Town football team's playing abode.)
'I'll happily take you, I like you, a lot
my name is Blue Mucus, I go like a shot.'
Joan says, 'Bon voyage', and Tony, 'Goodbye'
God says, 'Good riddance' and then starts to cry
Gus says, 'Good gracious, do you think you could try
and send us a postcard,' his eyes too are damp,
he gives them a moo and the price of a stamp.
So rider and horse set their course for the hills
as God starts displaying his footballing skills.
Blue Mucus comes in at a hundred to one
and then she collapses her laps is all run.
John takes a shovel and heaves at the ground
and leaves her dug into a dignified mound.
The spuds would have loved it
but they're not around.
He buries the horse in a plot
under the pitch on a penalty spot.
The groundswoman isn't amused
she believes the facility's being abused.
John says, 'I think it was right
to bury her bones at the end of her flight.'
'I've had enough of your gall,'
the official announces, 'I'm going to call

the police' but she doesn't she's hit by a ball.
It falls from the sky like some travelling bread
like manna from heaven, but hard on the head.
'If it were a spanner or ingot of lead
it would be worse,' she says rubbing the red
'but because it's a ball, made of leather instead
there's plenty of give and I'm able to live,'
she proudly announces before dropping dead.
John gets her buried alongside the steed,
food for the earth she was going to feed
and then sets off walking, he wants to locate
his father in Luton, before it's too late,
the father who gave him the juvenile pain
the thing he comes back to again and again.
But there's time for reflection conducting the search
he remembers his father was left in a church
and at last when they meet he is empty of blame
and he's able to say, 'I am glad that I came.
You gave me grief but now I understand,
you were unloved because you were unplanned
Dad, I forgive you, now give me your hand.'
Our tempers are short but our blood is still wet
we can still sort it out I am willing to bet
and I must buy a postcard don't let me forget.
You hurt me the same as your father hurt you
but for all of your hurting your heart remained true,
now the hurting must end,
   happy journey to you
   happy journey to you
   happy journey dear Daddy
   happy journey to you.'
'What's going on in there?' Somebody calls.

It's the dog that inhabits these sizeable walls,
'I must get a door with a lock and a key,
can someone say when'll my kennel be free?
Everyone out, of whatever renown
I've finished my dinner, I want a lie down.
I'm here with my dozen who've come from afar,
I'm going to explain to you who they all are:
one's very bubbly, her name is Spittle
one's been knocked over, we call her The Skittle
one's very snappy, referred to as Brittle,
one is called Mark,
one has no bark but she's able to neigh
she lives in a stable, she likes eating hay
she's a horse in a dog's body as you might say,
one is called Shaggy
one is called Kaggy he has a kagool
one has a stick that's still part of a stool
one is called Kitchen, he's shaped like a kettle
one's very restless she can't ever settle
one is called Rusty, she's oxidised metal
and one is called Nosey because he has got
a tail with two nostrils right over his bot
and he sniffs himself whether he wants to or not.'

Tony re-enters beginning to weep,
'The one of my dreams disappeared in my sleep
she left me, but left me with so much to keep,
she left me forever and left in a jeep.'
And all of a sudden the kennel's a squeeze
Tony and John they are back on their knees,
the two of them buckle, the two of them bend
they're back on their knees in a world where you tend

to find that what rises will also descend
where you wash with a flannel and watch what you
    spend
where a cow and a person don't commonly blend
where a kennel's a kennel and that's the end of it.
And that's the end of it.